Working with R.V.W.

DATE

A page from R.V.W.'s manuscript of *The First Nowell*
This, a particularly 'clean' sample, is the last complete page he ever
wrote (see p. 55)

Working with R.V.W.

ROY DOUGLAS

LONDON
OXFORD UNIVERSITY PRESS
NEW YORK TORONTO
1972

Oxford University Press, Ely House, London W.1

GLASGOW NEW YORK TORONTO MELBOURNE WELLINGTON
CAPE TOWN IBADAN NAIROBI DAR ES SALAAM LUSAKA ADDIS ABABA
DELHI BOMBAY CALCUTTA MADRAS KARACHI LAHORE DACCA
KUALA LUMPUR SINGAPORE HONG KONG TOKYO

ISBN 0 19 315427 7

© Oxford University Press 1972

Printed in Great Britain by
C. Tinling & Co. Ltd, London and Prescot

Prelude

From 1944 to 1958 I was closely associated with Ralph Vaughan Williams and his music, helping to prepare most of his major works, including the last four symphonies, for performance and publication. On the whole my task – though sometimes exhausting both mentally and physically – was absorbingly interesting, and I am happy in the knowledge that my assistance was of some considerable value and comfort to R.V.W. For me it was a labour of love in the sincerest meanings of both of those overworked words.

To music lovers who share my enthusiasm for the works of Vaughan Williams I offer this personal account of my years with him, presenting some hitherto unrecorded aspects of his processes of working, and many sidelights on the personality of a friend whose loss I felt more keenly than the loss of any other.

I have always found it difficult to choose the exact word to describe my position in relation to the composer: copyist is very inadequate; editor too pretentious; collaborator inaccurate; amanuensis is nearer. At one time I coined the phrase 'musical midhusband', as my job was to assist the composer in bringing his creations into the world of music.

Someone once asked me: 'Did you apply for the job?' Presumably the questioner imagined that it was a collaboration like that of Delius and Fenby. But my association with R.V.W. was not remotely comparable. Two questions I am more frequently asked are: 'How did you start working with Vaughan Williams?' and: 'When did you first meet him?' These are not easy to answer because the first time I helped to prepare some of his music I did not work with him, nor did I meet him, and it is possible that he never knew anything about it.

1941-1942 Film Music

In 1941 Vaughan Williams finished composing music for the film *49th Parallel*, and when the scores were sent to the copyists of the band parts they had much difficulty in reading his manuscript. His friends and relations were only too well aware that his handwriting was not easy to decipher, and his musical writing was usually just as illegible. He was ruefully conscious of the difficulty his writing caused, and used to joke about it himself; for instance, in 1951 he wrote to me concerning *Sinfonia Antartica:*

Dear Roy,

The new Symphony has now got far enough for me to want to hear you play it over to me. Would it be possible for you to come one day and do so? I have a very rough full score and a short score which is in my best handwriting, which you know. I think it is legible although not pretty.

His scores for *49th Parallel* must have been neither legible nor pretty, for the puzzled copyists made a great number of misreadings and wrong guesses, and I was told that at the first three-hour recording session almost the entire time was taken up with correcting wrong notes in the band parts. This annoyed the film company because it wasted their money, and film companies consider they have better ways of wasting money than on the unnecessary luxury of music. The musical director sent a strong complaint to the copying bureau, with the result that when, in the following year, V.W. wrote the music for another film, *Coastal Command*, the offended copyists refused to have anything to do with the scores. This created a problem for the film company, and eventually it was suggested that perhaps somebody could be found who would 'make the scores more readable' (a delightful euphemism) and this task was offered to me.

I have never known who recommended me, though several people have claimed that honour; I think it most likely that Gordon Walker put forward my name. Gordon was principal flute of the London Symphony Orchestra, and he and I were old friends and colleagues, for I also was a member of the L.S.O. I joined the orchestra in 1934 and was their pianist, organist, celesta-player, librarian, and fourth percussion for about ten years. Gordon also knew me to be a minor composer, as he had taken part in some of my chamber music and in some of the incidental music which I had written for broadcasts and films; more to the point, he was aware that I had something of a reputation for scoring my own and other people's music. I give these brief details about my background merely as evidence of the varied experience in playing and writing music which was so valuable in the work I was later to undertake for V.W.

When I looked at the scores of *Coastal Command* I

was considerably dismayed: this was my first sight of V.W.'s manuscript, and my eyes goggled and my mind boggled more than a little. After a while I decided that the only way to make the scores 'more readable' would be to write the whole lot out again after deciphering them; but there was not time to do this, because after I had finished the scores the copyists would have to write out the band parts, and the recording sessions were in a couple of days' time. So I embarked on the only practical course: copying out all the band parts myself.

It was rather noble of me to do this, for copying band parts is not a job one accepts with any enthusiasm: it can be very tedious, and is far from rewarding either artistically or financially. However, in this instance there was the unusual interest of dealing with brand new music straight from the pen of Vaughan Williams, and it was all in a good cause, so copy the parts I did. I wish I could round off the story by saying that at the recording session there were no wrong notes in the band parts, but I was not there and nobody told me what happened. And I doubt whether anyone told V.W. who had been 'making his scores more readable'.

1942: First Meeting

Such was my first practical encounter with the music of Vaughan Williams. The next came in September 1942 when I tackled the problem of fitting some sound tracks of his film music to a short film called *Young Farmers*.

I had still not met the composer, and as far as I knew he was not even aware of my existence, so I was very surprised when, in December 1942, I received a postcard in an unfamiliar and remarkable handwriting. I was able to make out the signature as 'R. V-squiggle W-squiggle', and the address as 'The White Gates, Dorking' with a telephone number; apart from these details all I could decipher was that he wanted me to ring him up about something. So I telephoned him and enquired – I hope tactfully – what the subject of the card was, and made an appointment to go over to Dorking. I must admit that I was very nervous at the prospect of meeting the great man; although I was thirty-five at the time, I suddenly felt very young and inexperienced, and rather like a small boy going to see the headmaster. Many years later Ursula Vaughan Williams, his second wife, told me that V.W. was probably feeling nervous too, as he was often shy of musicians whom he had not met before.

When I arrived at The White Gates V.W. welcomed me very politely, and we talked of the weather and of my train journey from Tunbridge Wells. Then, after a while, he asked almost casually: 'Did you go to the Royal College of Music or the Academy?' This question made me feel even more embarrassed, for at that time I was very self-conscious about the fact that – unlike most of my colleagues and rivals in the musical profession – I had received no academic training. So I answered shamefacedly: 'Neither; I'm afraid I'm one of those dreadful people, a self-taught musician.' His unexpected response to this was: 'Thank God for that. I get very tired of these young men from the College who think they know everything.' After that, I felt a little more relaxed, and we settled down to the main object of my visit, which was 'to give him a lesson' – this was a phrase he sometimes used to describe the occasions when he asked other musicians for advice (Gordon Jacob was one of those most frequently consulted).

The notion of this famous seventy-year-old composer seeking instruction from an obscure musician exactly half his age might seem unlikely and almost absurd. But throughout his long life V.W. was always eager to learn from anyone who could enlighten him on some aspect of music hitherto unfamiliar to him. In this instance he had been told that I might be able to give him information about certain 'tricks of the trade' in connection with scoring music for film sound tracks; in those days some combinations of instruments were more effective than others for recording purposes, and it was useful for a composer to know about such refinements of technique. I did my best to impart to him some of these secrets. Then he showed me the scores which he had written for his next film (this was either *The People's Land* or *Flemish Farm*), and I suggested a few minor alterations here and there to improve the clarity of texture for the sound track. After we finished the 'lesson' we had tea; I then returned to Tunbridge Wells, and heard no more from him for nearly two years.

1944-1945: Thanksgiving for Victory

Then, in October 1944, I received a letter from V.W. which said:

Dear Mr. Roy Douglas,

I understand from Peterkin of the O.U.P. that you might be willing to make a reduced score of the 'Victory Anthem' that I am writing for the B.B.C.

He had been invited by the B.B.C. to compose a work to celebrate the end of the war – doubtless they had received a Message From Above that we were going to win in the following year. V.W. responded with his *Thanksgiving for Victory*, later renamed *Song of Thanksgiving*, which he scored for a very large orchestra including six clarinets, six trumpets, two timpanists with six timpani between them, two harps, and organ. The Oxford University Press felt that, after the first performances, future concert promoters would be reluctant to go to the expense of engaging such a large number of players, so they suggested that perhaps the scoring could be reduced to make it possible to perform the work with a normal-sized symphony orchestra. I presume they had asked V.W. to do this himself, but he was doubtless already busy on his next major work; so Norman Peterkin had recommended that I should be invited to take on the task. Peterkin was the O.U.P. Music Editor, for whom I had already done a few jobs of arranging. I discussed the matter with V.W. and settled down to the reduction of the scoring; this entailed redistributing the parts for the 'extra' instruments so that they could be played by others – really what might be termed 'de-orchestration'.

When I submitted the new score to V.W. he showed much interest in some of my cunning devices, particularly those for dispensing with the third trumpet, and I was naturally delighted that he obviously approved of the work I had done. On looking back, I think he must have been more favourably impressed than I realized at the time, and it was perhaps at this point that he decided I might be able to help him in other ways; though he could not have foreseen, any more than I, that this was to be the start of fourteen years of working closely together.

Towards the end of 1945 V.W. conducted a performance of *Thanksgiving for Victory* in Dorking Church, for which he probably used a different reduced version which he had earlier asked me to prepare. He had a lifelong affection for amateur choirs in small towns and villages, and liked to make his choral works available for them to perform. Experience had taught him that small towns can seldom afford to engage large orchestras, but that they can usually rustle up a body of string players, so he used to provide alternative versions of these works to make it possible to perform them in churches with strings and organ, plus any trumpets or timpani which might be around. The new version was sometimes prepared by V.W. himself, but more often – as in this instance – it was done by some other musician under his supervision.

After I completed this job, in May 1945, I heard nothing more from him for the rest of that year or for the following year. This did not surprise me; I merely assumed that a brief but pleasant chapter in my musical life had ended. It had been a memorable experience to meet the great musician and to work with him a couple of times, but I had no reason to expect that I would ever work with him again. Nor was I unduly disturbed by the thought that we might not meet again, for there was no friendly relationship between us at that time. I was still not entirely at ease in his company, partly because I had not mastered the feeling of being overawed by his position of eminence as the greatest living British composer, and partly because his somewhat gruff manner and slightly forbidding appearance were rather terrifying at first – only later did one see the twinkle in his eye and realize his own shyness. I feel reasonably certain that, at the same time, V.W. was still a little nervous of me in a way: he had the idea that I was an expert on the subject of orchestration, and I think that for quite a long time he was afraid I might disapprove of his unconventional methods of scoring. Unconventional they were indeed, but his methods of scoring are, of course, part of what makes his music sound like that of no other composer.

So there remained this barrier of reserve between us, and we had not really got to know one another. Significant is the fact that our letters at this time still started: 'Dear Dr. Vaughan Williams' and 'Dear Mr. Douglas'.

1947: Sixth Symphony

Then, entirely unexpectedly, in February 1947 came a letter which started with slightly less formality:

Dear Douglas,

I have been foolish enough to write another symphony. Could you undertake to vet and then copy the score? If in the course of this you have any improvements to suggest I would receive them with becoming gratitude.

On March 10 Michael Mullinar is playing through the sketch at room 46 R.C.M. at 11.30 and 2.30 – could you (if you are able to undertake the work) come and hear it one of those times?

For some reason the play-through did not take place until 10 June, when I went along to the Royal College of Music together with forty or fifty other privileged persons, and there we heard for the first time the music of Vaughan Williams's Symphony in E minor, the one now known as No. 6. Mullinar played a piano arrangement of the work – in masterly fashion – while John Barbirolli and I followed the only MS full score. After the final desolate chords had faded *niente* there was a rapt silence: then Barbirolli said very quietly: '. . . Thank you.' Clearly he was as deeply moved as I – and surely all those present – by this powerful and disturbing work. Malcolm Sargent followed the score during a second play-through, and as soon as the symphony ended he reacted with his customary flamboyance, loudly crying 'Bravo!' and announcing that he wanted to conduct it as soon as possible.

In the afternoon the untiring Mullinar played the work twice more, for the benefit of Sir Adrian Boult, who was to conduct the first performance. Sir Adrian, with characteristic unselfishness, propped the score on a music-stand (which he insisted on fetching himself) so that four other people could follow it with him.

After thus hearing the work four times in one day, V.W. took the score home, saying that he 'had a lot of homework to do on it'; this meant that he would make various alterations in the score, perhaps cutting a few bars here and there, or entirely rewriting passages of the music. A month later he wrote to me again saying:

Herewith Full Score and Pfte arrangement of Symph.
Please (1) correct all actual errors of notes, etc.
         (2) correct all obvious errors of judgment.
         (3) all other cases which may be a matter of opinion but

which you think are wrong make a list and from time to time I shall value your opinion very much though I do not promise to accept your advice!

Having done this to have the score copied under your supervision (or alternatively to copy it yourself). I feel very happy leaving it in your expert hands.

With his usual thoughtfulness he left me a loophole of escape if I did not really want to copy it myself. Incidentally, the O.U.P. were partly behind this scheme of getting me to prepare a new score. Apparently a great deal of time had been wasted at the first rehearsal of V.W.'s Fifth Symphony in correcting wrong notes in the band parts, as the copyists had worked from his MS score, and O.U.P. doubtless thought that, with a more readable score of No. 6, there was a better chance of getting more accurate band parts.

So now I started on my first really big job for V.W. My diary records that I dealt with about sixteen bars a day, which perhaps seems a very small number, but it does represent about four pages of full score, which had to be written particularly carefully as they were intended for photographic reproduction. Further complications were: correcting 'all errors of notes' (by no means easy at times, especially as the symphony was in a Vaughan Williams idiom with which I was not then familiar); correcting 'all errors of judgment' (even more difficult – who was I to set up my judgement against his?); deciphering the manuscript, for I was not yet so adept at this as I later became. Also it was an extremely hot summer. The smaller errors and omissions were comparatively simple to correct, but there were also a great many little problems for which I was unable to find the answers myself; I made longish

lists of these, and either sent them by post or took them to
Dorking where we sorted out the answers together. I
always felt a little guilty during these sessions, for I could
see that it bored V.W. to have to go over all these finicking
little details, but he endured the task patiently, though
occasionally during a hot afternoon he would 'drop off'
for two or three minutes and, on waking, resume exactly
where we had left off, apparently unconscious that his
eyes had even closed.

'All Actual Errors'

For those who are interested in knowing something of the
kind of little puzzles I had to solve, here is part of an
article which I wrote for the *R.C.M. Magazine* in 1959:
'He wrote his scores in ink and apparently very quickly,
and many unintentional discrepancies found their way
on to the pages. Small things such as a missing bass clef
after a tenor, *arco* missing after *pizz.*, "change to flute 2"
missing after piccolo, clarinets in A mistransposed as if in
B flat, trumpet passages written on the horns' line for a
few bars – all these were easily put right. At times,
however, the complete woodwind or brass section or
timpani would be playing up to the end of a right-hand
page and over the page there would be blank bars; in
these instances I would pencil-in what I thought he might
have intended as continuation and send it to him. Sometimes my guess was right, and sometimes entirely wrong.
Again, perhaps one of those curious scale-passages would

have a G sharp in all the wind and a G natural in all the
strings when it was quite obvious that they ought to be the
same. On consulting the piano score I might find that it
had F, or A, and not G at all: another query for the
composer to answer. There were also occasions when I
just could not read the notes. My favourite instance of
this was in *Hodie*. I tried one unlikely-looking clarinet
passage in B flat and in A, wondered if it had strayed
from the cor anglais line or the bassoon (in tenor or in
bass clef), but eventually had to give it up and ask him
what the notes were meant to be; the reply came back:
"Can't make this out at all, let's leave it out." And we
did. . . .

. . . R.V.W. allowed me to refashion his harp, piano and
xylophone parts because he liked to think that I could
improve the layout for the pedals, fingers and sticks, thus
making the parts more enjoyable for the players.'

On consulting my diary I am somewhat surprised to find
that I succeeded in completing the new copy of the full
score in a couple of months, and delivered it to V.W. in
the middle of September 1947; in my innocence I thought
that this would be the end of my work on the symphony.
However, in November V.W. wrote to say he had made a
few more changes; many of these were merely adjustments
of the expression marks to improve the balance between
the instruments – his constant concern was that the
important things in the score should be clearly heard.
Several of the changes were more drastic, and some of
my beautiful pages of score had to be completely rewritten. When I had finished revising the score, the
O.U.P. copyists wrote out the band parts, and all was
prepared for the first orchestral run-through in December;

this was given by the B.B.C. Symphony Orchestra with Sir Adrian. I am delighted to say that at this rehearsal the orchestra did not once have to stop to correct wrong notes in the band parts.

After this run-through, I assumed that I now really had finished my work on the score, but again I was wrong. Very soon after hearing the symphony played by an orchestra V.W. decided to make further small changes, and I had to see that these alterations were made in all the newly photographed copies of the full score, and to supervise the revision of the band parts. This took me until 2 January. At last everything was ready for the first performance, which was at the Albert Hall in April 1948.

It was at one of the Albert Hall rehearsals that I was made aware that I had an additional duty, and a somewhat alarming one on its first manifestation. Several times Boult asked the composer about the balance of the texture, but V.W.'s hearing was becoming unreliable by then: sometimes it was surprisingly acute, but at other times neither of his hearing aids (not even the one he nicknamed his 'coffee-pot') was of much help. Eventually, in response to an inquiry from Sir Adrian, he said: 'I can't hear anything. You'll have to ask Roy Douglas.' I then found myself, to my great embarrassment, having to address the conductor across the wide open spaces of the Albert Hall, conscious that everyone's eyes and ears were upon me – the entire orchestra and the forty or fifty people who were sparsely dotted around the auditorium. This incident made me realize that V.W. was having to rely on me as an 'extra pair of ears', and that it was my responsibility to decide on these matters of balance.

The Sixth Symphony was warmly praised, especially

for its power and vigour, by the critics, though a few of them angered V.W. by insisting that it depicted 'war and subsequent desolation', in spite of irate denials by him of any such intention. I asked him what he thought about this 'War Symphony' suggestion, and his reply was: 'I suppose it never occurs to these people that a man might just want to write a piece of music.'

1950: Folk Songs of the Four Seasons

After this first performance there was no more work for me with V.W. during 1948, and for the rest of the year I was occupied with revising and correcting the full score of Walton's *Belshazzar's Feast* in preparation for its photographic reproduction. During the whole of 1949 also there was complete silence from V.W. as far as I was concerned, though there were occasional rumours from O.U.P. of 'another major work in preparation'. But, before this materialized, I had a couple of sizable jobs to do for him. In March 1950 he asked me to 'vet' and write out a new score of his cantata *Folk Songs of the Four Seasons* for women's voices and orchestra, which was performed in June at the Albert Hall by three thousand members of Women's Institutes, with Boult and the L.S.O.

In connection with this work, I remember arriving with V.W. and Ursula at the Royal Festival Hall for a rehearsal of a later performance; at the front entrance dozens of ladies of the choir were standing around, seemingly to give the composer a hero's welcome; on seeing them, V.W. looked dismayed and said hastily: 'Can't we go in the back way?' And we did so. This example of his distaste for public acclaim reminds me of an incident which occurred after he had conducted a performance of his *London Symphony*; the applause recalled him several times, and as he left the stage for the fourth or fifth time he whispered something to the orchestra's leader. Those present assumed that he had made some complimentary remark about the playing of the orchestra, but what he really said was: 'Why do they keep on calling me back; are my fly-buttons undone or something?'

During the preparation of the Sixth Symphony my long lists of errors and omissions seemed to come as rather a shock to the composer, who had presumably not quite realized just how much his scores did need 'vetting'. I therefore resolved to worry him as little as possible with queries about the *Folk Songs of the Four Seasons*, but inevitably there were a number of problems which I was unable to solve myself. In reply to one of my queries he wrote:

Dear Douglas,

I am ashamed of myself – 'Pure carelessness, sir' as Dr. Johnson said. What I evidently did was I started in a routine way marking 'Trb and Tuba' – then found no use for the Tuba and forgot to mark it out. Also please make the harp passages into harp music.

The adaptation of a remark by Dr. Johnson cropped up many times in his letters during the ensuing years, and he often used to say regretfully 'I'm afraid I'm incorrigibly careless'. These innumerable small errors were not really caused by carelessness in the sense of 'not bothering'; they were more the result of his very agile mind running away with his pen – something which happens to many composers. Apart from the creative aspect of writing a full score, the actual physical labour is long and tedious, necessitating hundreds of thousands of separate movements of the pen, and it is very easy for a composer to miss the insertion of small but important details – such as *arco*, *senza sordini*, or a change of clef – in the string parts when his attention has switched to the balancing of the wind parts. Also V.W. would frequently change the harmonies, or the notes in scale-like passages, while scoring a work, and would make these alterations perhaps in the strings, forgetting that he had left the passages in the wind as they had been in his reduced score or piano sketch. As I have already indicated, it was part of my job to spot all these little discrepancies and put them right, or query them with the composer; this naturally required a considerable amount of concentration, and was very tiring mentally. I should not like to claim that I corrected every single error in his scores, especially in the early days of my work with him, but I eventually came to reckon myself as being capable of 99½% accuracy.

The other work I dealt with about this time was his *Fantasia on the Old 104th* for pianoforte solo with chorus and orchestra; and while I was coping with this the secret of the 'major work in preparation' was disclosed.

1950-1951: The Pilgrim's Progress

Early in July 1950 V.W. asked me if I was willing to help in my usual way with *The Pilgrim's Progress*, his new four-act opera – or 'Morality', as he preferred to call it. I wish I could say that I felt overjoyed at the thought of helping him with such a large-scale work, but honesty compels me to admit that my first reaction was not entirely of pleasure. My musical life was at that time interestingly varied: tidying up works by sundry British composers, arranging and scoring music of all kinds and periods for different publishers, and sometimes finding time to compose some of my own. Now I was faced with the prospect of restricting my activities to one work by one composer, certainly for many months ahead, possibly even for a year or so. In my reply to V.W. I hoped I had concealed my slight reluctance, but he must have sensed something of it, for when he wrote on 12 July (now addressing me as 'Dear Roy Douglas'), thanking me for my 'expert advice' on some rescoring he had done in *Hugh the Drover*, he added: 'As regards my Opera, I have a feeling that you do not want to do it, and it occurred to me the reason was that you wanted time for your own composition. If you have any inspiration floating about it would certainly be blasphemy against the Holy Ghost to interfere with it, and I should not like to be a party to that; so think it over carefully before you decide.'

Such unselfishness and readiness to suggest that I should place my interests before his own were very characteristic of the man. It was then, I think, that I must have come to terms with myself and decided that I, too, should be prepared to make sacrifices; after all, my small talent for composing and my gift for arranging music were relatively unimportant, and I would be of more service to the cause of music by henceforth devoting most of my energies to helping Vaughan Williams.

It took me thirty-three weeks to write out the full score of *Pilgrim's Progress*, from August to the following March, being somewhat hampered by the fact that, by the time I was working on the second Act, V.W. was already rewriting parts of Act I, and similarly with the later acts. In addition, a number of changes had to be made for stage purposes as the production developed. For instance, in November he wrote:

Dear Douglas,

I am going to be a nuisance (which you probably are not surprised at!) Here is an 'appendix' for Act I (I expect the opera will suffer from a good deal of appendicitis before we have done with it). It consists of a few additional bars before figure 10 . . . etc. . . .

In April I attended some of the rehearsals at Covent Garden. These were mostly very unsatisfactory, for the orchestra usually rehearsed without the singers, and the cast rehearsed on the stage with piano only. A note from V.W. to me ends disgustedly: 'C. Garden on Tuesday, orchestra only 12.30–1.30. The rest with pfte (or banjo? or harmonium?)'

It was during these rehearsals that I first met Sir Gilmour Jenkins, a close friend of V.W. and Ursula for many years; Gil and I came to know one another very well after this, meeting often at V.W.'s house and at rehearsals, and always at first performances.

I could cover several pages with an account of the trials and tribulations we (that is, V.W., Ursula, and I) went through during the preparation of the production, but one incident must suffice, and I choose this because it gives an example of V.W.'s quick response to an amusing situation. In Act IV 'the Voice of a Bird' is heard off stage; V.W. advised from the start that the soprano should be placed in the orchestra pit and the three Shepherds be asked to look upwards: this, he said, would cheat the audience into imagining she was up in the trees. His excellent sense of stagecraft was always to be relied on, but the stage staff took no notice and stationed her in one place after another in the wings without success. After wasting about forty-five minutes they tried his suggestion, and the illusion was as he had predicted and – equally important – the singer could now see the conductor. Only one thing disturbed V.W.: each Shepherd seemed to be looking up a different tree, and he said quietly to us: 'I wish they'd make up their minds which tree she's barking up.'

At last, on 26 April 1951, came the long-awaited first performance. Long awaited indeed, for Vaughan Williams had loved and admired John Bunyan's allegory for most of his life, and for forty years or more had been planning this wedding of his music to Bunyan's words for a stage representation. Alas, the production was a lamentable failure. Musically the standard of performance was reasonably good – V.W. had nothing but praise for the young conductor, Leonard Hancock, and for many of the singers. But the scenery and costumes, the staging, lighting, and production generally – all these fell far short of the composer's conception.

It is, I am sure, true to say that this shabby miscreation of his beloved *Pilgrim's Progress* was the bitterest disappointment of his musical life, and those of us who were close to him at the time felt very sad to see him so despondent. Fortunately he was comforted three years later by seeing some performances of an excellent production by Dennis Arundell at Cambridge.

Very soon after the first performances V.W. was busy with 'alterations and repairs', and during the remainder of 1951 I was not surprised to receive at intervals post-cards and letters (I was now addressed as 'Dear Roy') containing details of revisions. All of these I naturally had to deal with: putting them into the full scores and making sure that they were correctly inserted in the band parts. At the same time I was correcting some of the proofs of the 236 pages of the vocal score for publication. I finished these jobs on *Pilgrim's Progress* in January 1952.

Problems of Balance

In the midst of all this I had found time to help V.W. with another small task. He wrote in September 1951:

Dear Roy,

As there seem to be about to be a good many performances of my symphonies I think they ought to be overhauled. I am sending you 'Pastoral' and 'No. 5' – will you help me by going through them carefully and suggesting alterations in any places where in your opinion the texture (and especially the orchestra-tion) does not 'come off'. It is often difficult to decide whether one ought to score for the wireless, the concert room, or the Albert Hall – also I am getting deaf and things which are probably all right sound all wrong to me.

It would be safe to say that he almost invariably scored for the concert hall, and he was therefore fre-quently disappointed by broadcasts and recordings; in

1951 these media were of course far less highly developed than they are today. Even now the balance of sound in a work can be distorted by the twiddling of knobs by engineers. Some of the excellent modern recordings would perhaps have satisfied even V.W.; but, because of their complexity and the large forces employed, it would still seem virtually impossible to obtain a truly satisfactory balance in a broadcast performance of his big choral works such as *Hodie* and *Sancta Civitas*.

The fact that he made so many alterations to a work after hearing it – even many years afterwards, as in the cases of the *Pastoral* and Fifth Symphony – might give the impression that V.W. was a bungler and didn't know what he was doing. Nothing could be further from the truth. He knew what he was doing and why he wanted to do it – indeed, I would describe him as a perfectionist, though he might not have thought of himself as such. In his mind he could 'auralize' (a word coined on the analogy of 'visualize') the ideal orchestral balance that was required for his music to be heard as he had conceived it, and that is why he would go to such infinite trouble in trying to get the smallest details to his satisfaction; it is also why he was often so disheartened to find that a work which sounded as he wanted it in one concert hall could sound wrongly balanced in another, and why he was disturbed by the distortions which frequently resulted from transmission by a microphone. The description which has sometimes been given of V.W. as a clumsy amateur whose scoring was thick and incompetent is wildly inaccurate, and those people who disparage his music by merely repeating such foolish charges should really do their homework by studying his scores, any of which will provide examples of most delicate and imaginative orchestration.

1952: Sinfonia Antartica

In November 1951 I had visited V.W. at Dorking to discuss some problems concerning *Pilgrim's Progress*, and while I was there he had shown me the score of the first movement of a work which he had nearly finished: this was the *Sinfonia Antartica*. In January 1952 I went over to Dorking to play the complete symphony to V.W. and Ursula; and three weeks later I played it again, this time in Alan Frank's office at the O.U.P., to a small group of people consisting of V.W., Ursula, Sir Arthur Bliss, the composer Gerald Finzi, who was a very dear friend of V.W. for many years, and Alan Frank, the head of music of the O.U.P. Not unexpectedly V.W. had made alterations since I had played it at Dorking, and I found myself confronted with a copy decorated with several strips of music-paper each containing half a page, a line, or even a couple of bars, stuck on (slightly askew) with thick yellow sticky tape, and an odd bit here and there – just a bar or so – added in some corner of a page with an arrow pointing to where it should be inserted.

At this stage in the development of a new work V.W. found these play-throughs extremely helpful. When a composer has spent many months of intensive work on all the details of his creation, it becomes very difficult for him to stand back and view the work as a whole. By the time he had written the 'fair copy' of the full score, V.W. was usually in a curiously ambivalent state of mind: on the one hand he had sufficient confidence in his new work to consider it worthy of being brought before the public, and on the other he was not entirely free from doubts as to its intrinsic value. This made him genuinely nervous on the occasion when works were first played to his friends, a fact which he endeavoured to hide by using turns of speech which were an endearing mixture of humorous mock-modesty and earnest anxiety. He would sometimes preface a play-through by saying: 'I want to see whether there's anything worth keeping'; and after I had finished he would often look at us over his spectacles almost apprehensively and ask: 'Is it all right, do you think?' Reassurances would follow, and then he would discuss a few adjustments of speed, perhaps talk of 'cutting out some of the dead wood', or ask if we thought a certain passage was 'a bit too much like Joseph Barnby or Caleb Simper' – he sometimes loved to pretend that the sickly chromaticism of these two Victorian composers (whose works seemed to have a horrid fascination for him) had influenced his music!

After the play-through of *Sinfonia Antartica*, V.W. took the score away to do his usual 'homework'. Meanwhile I busied myself with some work on his *Folk Songs of the Four Seasons*; this was a reduced scoring of the wind parts for a special performance which was to be given with a smaller orchestra.

Returning to this score after a couple of years, I was

charmed afresh by many of his settings of the folk-songs, and I conceived the idea of making an orchestral suite from some of the most attractive and suitable movements. R.V.W. and O.U.P. approved, and I set to work. When I had planned the sequence of movements, I took the sketch to V.W. and he gave it his blessing – with one reservation: I had devised several modulations (which I thought rather ingenious) to join the tunes together. He asked me to remove some of these, as he disliked modulations in principle; he preferred to move abruptly from one key to another. Incidentally, I took a delight in turning the tables on him three years later. Towards the very end of his Eighth Symphony there were a couple of bars of modulation which I felt were unconvincing; I plucked up the courage to tell him so, and he soon decided to cut them out and jump straight into the new key. Examples of his use of 'jump-cuts' in preference to modulations can be found in many of his later works; in some instances they occur where he had cut some bars to tighten up the structure of a movement.

My Suite was published and is occasionally performed, though not as often as I could wish, for V.W. had – with characteristic generosity – insisted that I should receive the lion's share of the royalties.

On 23 April 1952 V.W. wrote:

Dear Roy,

I feel I have done all I can now with the S.A. so it must now take its chance. .... As you know it wants its face washing badly. Will you undertake this?

And on 5 June I received a brief note, the first sentence of which I have never yet succeeded in deciphering; the second sentence reads: 'I fear S.A. will want a good deal of washing.' 'S.A.' is obviously *Sinfonia Antartica*, and 'washing its face' is a phrase which he often used to describe my ministrations.

When playing the symphony on the piano I had quickly spotted that the rising chords at the very opening of the work were uncomfortably reminiscent of a passage in Elgar's *In the South* (in an Antarctic Symphony, too!) I was reluctant at first to point this out to V.W., but I eventually felt compelled to do so, and he wrote in reply: 'As regards "In the South" I did not deliberately quote it, but as soon as I had written it I knew what I had done, but decided it was what I wanted and must be kept. Nobody seems to have noticed it – though perhaps it only meant that they were too polite to say so! I have now looked it over carefully and I have decided that I can improve it, and also disappoint the witch hunters by a slight alteration. The only problem now is, have I made it more, rather than less like "In the South"?' The answer was, of course, less like.

In September I wrote asking him why he had omitted the names of the authors of the quotations which head the movements. His reply shows evidence of his care for practical details: 'As regards the authors of the quotations, I did not want to appear to be a prig, so I have decided to add them, they are as follows. . . . As regards the instrumentation, I am rather alarmed at the number of percussion players required. Could not the wind machine man be one of the four? . . . and rush behind the screen at the critical moment. Also, would it save a player if we could arrange the xylo and the glock should not play simultaneously? It would probably not hurt much. I have changed my mind about the soprano solo and chorus. They need not be out of sight, but should be either behind or in the middle of the orchestra, at all events not in front.' He later changed his mind again on this last point.

A month or so before his eightieth birthday he wrote:

Dear Roy,

Herewith your corrections of S.A. with my comments thereon. By the way, have you had an invitation to the party in Dorking in October 11 – and can you come? If so, I believe they are sending a concert ticket to all those who accept. If they do *not* will you let *me* know.

Yrs, R.V.W.

P.S. I am supposed to know nothing about the party.

1952: Manchester

From June 1952 onwards *Sinfonia Antartica* had kept me very busy; I had dealt with the usual corrections, consultations, and second thoughts, and had checked and corrected hundreds of pages of the band parts, completing all these tasks by the end of October.

On 24 November V.W., Ursula, and I went up to Manchester to hear the symphony rehearsed the following day by the Hallé Orchestra with Barbirolli, who were to give the first performance. This was certainly an experience to be remembered: we listened to a three-hour rehearsal by the wind-players only, from ten till one; then three hours of the strings only, from two till five; finishing up with three hours of the full orchestra, from six till nine; all taking place in a rehearsal room just large enough to accommodate the orchestra, the conductor, and the three listeners.

V.W.'s hearing was now sadly deteriorating, and he had increasingly to rely on me to decide on matters of balance between the various parts of the orchestra (his constantly reiterated question at rehearsals was: 'Does the tune come through?'); this meant that on this occasion I had to concentrate intently for nine hours with brief intervals, so it is not surprising that I finished the day something of an exhausted and bewildered wreck. Whereas V.W. seemed to be remarkably fresh and lively in mind at the end of the day. He had the very useful gift of being able to relax into a short sleep at almost any time (indeed, he had a brief nap during the afternoon rehearsal), and these little periods of physical and mental rest helped him, I believe, to preserve his amazing vitality.

When we returned to London there were the usual alterations to be made; in fact, there were a great many revisions in *Sinfonia Antartica*, because he had experimented with a wealth of new sound-colours in the orchestration, and he was determined to get these exactly as he wanted them. Every one of these alterations had to be made in the scores and band parts, and I finished work on all this just in time to take a well-earned rest at Christmas.

An Absurd Rumour

It was about this time that a most regrettable rumour began to circulate, to the effect that I was *orchestrating*

Vaughan Williams's music. Utterly ridiculous, of course; for one thing, he had been writing for orchestra for about forty years before I even met him (for instance, *Toward the Unkown Region*, which is very efficiently scored, was first performed in 1907 two days before I was born). Apart from that, V.W. – like any other true composer – could think orchestrally (that is, he could hear the sounds of the instruments in his imagination while he was composing), and it is inconceivable that Vaughan Williams – any more than Beethoven or Wagner – should need anyone else to orchestrate his music.

It is possible that V.W. himself may have been inadvertently responsible for the start of this rumour. He had a pet little joke which he liked to bring out concerning me. During a rehearsal of a new work, he often went on to the stage to confer with the conductor; on these occasions he used to take me with him and introduce me to the orchestra by saying: 'This is Mr. Roy Douglas who writes my music for me.' The players always greeted this with appreciative chuckles, for orchestral musicians know better than anyone whether a man scores his own works or not, and they were in no doubt whatever about V.W.'s ability to write and score his own music; they realized it was just one of his little jokes, and one assumed that everyone else within hearing took it in the same spirit. (This joke had been shared between the two of us for quite a long time; in a letter of 1947, concerning the Sixth Symphony, he had ended: '. . . Also to remind you that you have not yet sent in your a/c for the last bit which you composed of the symph.')

It may have been that someone who heard V.W.'s remark failed to understand that it was a joke, and

C

repeated it as a solemn statement of fact; or possibly someone said, purely in fun, 'You know, I suppose, that Roy Douglas orchestrates Vaughan Williams's music now?' without expecting to be taken seriously; or maybe, as I have sometimes suspected, some ill-disposed person started the rumour out of sheer malice. Whatever the circumstances of its origin, the stupid rumour spread in musical circles, and quickly acquired a more unpleasant aspect: gossip reported that I was actually *claiming* to orchestrate V.W.'s music. Indeed, I was obliquely attacked in a Sunday newspaper by a music critic who had been told that I was making such a claim.

Naturally, I was extremely upset by all this; not only was the rumour absurdly and even wickedly untrue, but also it was hurtful to me to think that anyone could suspect me of being so disloyal to V.W. Even more worrying was the possibility that, if the story had been taken seriously, it could have been injurious to V.W.'s reputation; unkind people might have started saying: 'Poor old chap, he's getting past it, and has to have someone to help him.'

I wrote to V.W. on the matter, because I couldn't bear the thought that he might hear about it and perhaps wonder if I had made some misunderstood remark which could have set the rumour off. He replied quite light-heartedly by saying: 'As regards the idea that you score my works from a sketch . . . the obvious answer is that if you had done so it would have sounded a great deal better'. This was another of his little jokes, of course – if I *had* scored his works they would undoubtedly have sounded different, but most emphatically not 'better'. What he omitted to say was that he had considerately written a long letter to Neville Cardus in 1953, clearly hoping that

Cardus, being an influential music critic, might be able to combat the foolish rumour. In the letter V.W. described some of the ways in which I helped him, and ended by saying: 'I am prepared to ignore all these idle tongues, but if the matter does crop up again, I owe it to Mr. Douglas to explain what happened. He earns his living by orchestration and I should not like him to be blamed for my shortcomings.' Bless his heart – what a thing to say!

I was not aware of this letter's existence until I read it ten years later in Michael Kennedy's book, where it is printed more fully; again typical of V.W. to do his good deeds by stealth.

Presumably because the story was too preposterous to be believed, the rumour faded out, and I have not heard anything of such nonsense for many years. There is, however, always a danger that it might be resurrected; some musicological busybody may discover that, in the hire library of the O.U.P., most of the full scores of V.W.'s later large-scale works are in my handwriting, and from this he may deduce wrongly that I orchestrated them. One can only hope that such a person will read this account of the work which I really did for V.W., and thus be prevented from making a fool of himself.

It will do no harm, I think, to repeat what Michael Kennedy says in his book about the Vaughan Williams full scores: 'It cannot be too strongly emphasized that the only trustworthy full scores of most of the later large-scale works ... are those in the handwriting of Roy Douglas and the printed scores which were engraved from these.' He then goes on to describe how, when alterations were made by the composer after a performance, the revisions were put into the photographed copies of my newly written scores, and were seldom added in the composer's MS scores. He continues: 'It is obvious, therefore, that the full scores in Vaughan Williams's handwriting, most of which are now in the British Museum, do not represent these works as the composer wished them to be performed.'

1953-1954: Hodie

After having issued that warning to posterity, I can now return to 1953. During much of that year my time was almost entirely occupied with various tasks concerning the music of William Walton, though I did fit in a couple of jobs for V.W.: one was the correcting of proofs of the full score of *Sinfonia Antartica*. He had also made his famous arrangement of *The Old Hundredth* for the Coronation, and I had to correct many copyists' mistakes in the band parts, which had been copied from his original MS score.

Early in August V.W. asked me to go over to Dorking to play through his new 'tune' – one of his quirks was to say of a recently completed work 'I have written a new tune', and the 'tune' could be anything from a Flourish for three trumpets to a full-scale symphony. This new work was his Christmas cantata *Hodie*, and he wanted me to run it through with him before the 'official' play-through. He wrote: 'The playing through on your part will involve faking up the thing to include solo and chorus parts where necessary. There is, or will be, a pianoforte arrangement nicely copied by Gus, and an illegible full score by me; you can use which you like.' (Gus was an invaluable copyist named Gustav de Mauny who did a lot of preliminary copying for V.W.)

A few days after going to Dorking I played the work at the R.C.M. to about twenty of his musical friends, including David Willcocks who was to conduct it at the Three Choirs Festival the following year. V.W. stood behind me while I was playing, reading the music over my shoulder and singing away happily throughout – all the solos, and the chorus parts whenever he could fit them in. Unfortunately for me – probably because he was a little keyed-up and over-anxious – there were moments when he missed a beat or so's rest and came in too soon; this made things somewhat awkward, for I had long experience as an accompanist, and my instinct bade me keep with the singer. Yet I was uncomfortably aware that, in doing so, I was distorting his music by skipping a beat now and then to keep up with him. But he was enjoying himself, and that was all that mattered!

During the ensuing months I received numerous letters containing revisions, instructions, suggestions, and queries. To give a few extracts: 'As regards the title, are you afraid people will call it "Howdy"?' (I had expressed doubts as to the wisdom of giving the work a Latin title; it seemed to me that people without a classical education – like myself – might be embarrassed at trying to pronounce it.) '... I fear that in spite of you I am going to add another verse to the worse-than-Delius-and-almost-as-bad-as-Barnby choral. I hope Ursula will do one.' (This is the penultimate unaccompanied choral in D flat, for which Ursula wrote a very ingenious second verse, using exactly the same rhymes as in the anonymous first verse. Presumably I had expressed some dislike for this movement – but surely I could not have been so outspoken as to compare it with Delius and Barnby!)

One very brief note I will quote here, though I am unable to date it accurately, as it is merely headed 'Jan 27' (he very seldom added the year, unluckily for the chronicler). It runs:

Dear Roy,

Here is something 'on account'. Let me know sometime what the total ought to be – though indeed the price of your wisdom is above rubies – unfortunately I haven't got any rubies.

V.W. moved in 1953 from Dorking to Hanover Terrace, Regent's Park, and in November I went to see him there to discuss the vocal score of *Hodie*, which I now had to prepare for publication by arranging the music so that it could be played by the average pianist; this took me a couple of months, which was not bad going, considering there were nearly 1300 bars in the work. After receiving a copy of this piano arrangement he wrote: 'Very many thanks. It flows so beautifully under even my hands that I can hardly believe it is mine. I hope I have answered all your queries intelligibly and intelligently.' (These were queries on the full score.)

From March to June 1954 I was busy 'washing the face' of the 200 pages of full score. When this was almost completed he wrote: 'Ursula is away, so you will have to put up with my cacography.' (Ursula often typed his letters – not very expertly, as she is the first to admit.) 'Now the score is nearly finished a new problem presents itself – I have an idea that this work is likely to become popular with school choral societies – but, as usual, I have made the orchestration (probably unnecessarily) elaborate and difficult – would you consider re-scoring it to bring it within the means of the average school orchestra.'

Of all the tasks which V.W. asked me to undertake, this was the only one which I felt unable to accept, as I was convinced that it was not a practical proposition. The string parts were full of very awkward intervals and rapid intricate passage-work, and I was sure that amateurs would find the notes almost unplayable. As a compromise I suggested arranging the score for two pianos and strings, giving the difficult passages to the pianos and inventing simpler parts for the strings, but he didn't like this idea at all. I felt rather guilty about all this, for he clearly wanted so much to have this simplified version, but I just could not take on a job which I was sure I could not do successfully; he continued to try to persuade me, but my reluctance and lack of confidence in the proposed scheme must at last have discouraged him, and the matter was allowed to drop.

'Lost without Gustav'

The most difficult letter to answer was one in which he asked me for any criticisms of *Hodie* as a work. I replied to this: 'I have been giving a good deal of thought to *Hodie* and have come to the conclusion that I'm not really very competent to give any useful criticisms or suggestions.

You see, when I'm fully occupied with trying to play the notes, I find it difficult to detach myself sufficiently to judge the work as music. However, there are one or two points which strike me.' (This was probably when I criticized the 'Delius-Barnby' movement.) I could have added that, by the time I had written out an entire full score, I found it even more hopeless to try to evaluate all those crotchets and quavers as a work of art – the cliché about the wood and the trees is inescapable.

Besides these entirely sincere reasons there was also a deeper one: I was often aware of how profoundly he missed being able to submit his new works to the unsparingly critical eye of his beloved friend Holst, who had died in 1934. Michael Kennedy quotes a letter which V.W. wrote to S. P. Waddington in 1952, in which he said: 'I feel lost without you and Gustav to look over my things and tell me where I get off. Nobody else has *both* the skill and the patience to tell me what I want to know.' When I read this in 1964, I felt very sad, for it made me realize that perhaps I could have given him some of the criticism and encouragement he craved, had I been more self-confident. I have no doubt whatever that I would have had the patience, but by no stretch of imagination could I have regarded myself as having the skill, musicianship, and judgement of such a rare spirit as Gustav Holst. To be fair to myself, I did on one occasion venture to express my doubts over the shape of a movement; this was the second movement of *Antartica*, of which I said I thought that, if it was a Scherzo, the recapitulation of the first part was perhaps too much shortened to be convincing. My suggestion was not at all well received, in fact this was probably the only time in the whole of our association when he appeared almost displeased with me. This understandably discouraged me from offering my opinion again, except on comparatively minor points.

Before I had finished work on *Hodie* I was given the score of his Tuba Concerto to deal with. Luckily this was a fairly short work, for it was needed in a frantic hurry, and I succeeded in 'washing its face' and writing out the 74 pages of full score in just under a fortnight.

After the first performance of *Hodie* at Worcester in September 1954, there were the now-expected revisions and alterations to be made. Just before he left for the U.S.A., V.W. wrote: 'You will curse me to my face, but I have done some re-scoring of *Hodie*. Will you put in the corrections for me and be an angel?' There was no great hurry for these to be done, and I had work of a more urgent nature for Walton at this time, so I didn't finish dealing with the *Hodie* revisions until early in January 1955, in good time for the first London performance on the 19th.

1955: Eighth Symphony

There was now silence from V.W. for nearly three months, but experience had taught me that silence on his part did not by any means denote inactivity; it was far more likely that another new 'tune' was being prepared. This was indeed the case, for on 1 April 1955 my diary records: 'R.V.W. rang; he has written another symphony.' (How

glad I am that I have kept diaries since 1922!) This was
a symphony in D, and as he had already written one
symphony in D – the one we know now as No. 5 – it was
suggested by O.U.P. and by me that he should call this
new one No. 8. But he had a strange objection to the
idea of numbering his symphonies. I pointed out in a
letter to him that, with two symphonies in D, it might
happen one day that some luckless orchestra might sit
down to play one of them and find themselves faced with
the band parts of the other. He replied: 'I have never put
numbers to my symphonies yet and I don't want to start
now. After all, Beethoven wrote a D major and a D minor,
and nobody seems much the worse, and it won't do much
harm if they do play number five instead of number
eight!'

I rather fancy that he weakened his position with that
last sentence, for to differentiate between the two he had
referred to them by numbers. In fact, he referred several
times to 'No. 5' in letters to me when he was revising it
during 1951. Eventually the O.U.P. succeeded in persuad-
ing a very reluctant V.W. to allow the new symphony
to be called No. 8.

On 4 April I played the symphony to V.W. and Ursula,
and a week later I played it again to a small gathering of
friends, chiefly musicians whose judgement he particularly
valued: this little group of people I privately nicknamed
'the inner circle'. On this occasion it consisted of V.W.
himself, Ursula, Arthur Bliss and Lady Bliss, Gerald
Finzi and his wife, the composers Edmund Rubbra
and Herbert Howells, the music critics Frank Howes and
Scott Goddard, and Alan Frank. I must confess that it
was something of an ordeal to play before this distinguished

assembly which included five eminent composers – one of whom was the Master of the Queen's Musick, two others being professors of composition – and a couple of important critics; however, I comforted myself with the thought that none of these gentlemen would be as proficient as I in reading V.W.'s manuscript.

Since the play-through of *Sinfonia Antartica* a kind of routine had developed for these occasions. Before I started V.W. would say that he wanted his friends to give candid opinions of the work and to suggest any improvements; adding: 'I always ask everybody's advice but never promise to take any of it.' This, according to him, was a favourite remark of Holst's.

What he wanted, I feel sure, from these knowledgeable and experienced musicians was the kind of advice and guidance that Holst had given him. He hoped they would be able to tell him whether the new work seemed worthy of taking its place among his other works which they knew and admired. Also he wanted to hear their opinions on the construction of the work as a whole, and on the balance between the various sections of each movement. The man who always provided the most perceptive and valuable judgements was Bliss. He was remarkably clever at grasping the shape of a symphonic movement and assessing the proportions of a work in its entirety on a first hearing; in fact, V.W. more than once made slight alterations to a movement in accordance with a suggestion by Bliss. It must not be thought that V.W. was willing to chop his music about to please anybody; when he was quite sure that a movement was exactly the right shape and its component sections justly balanced, it was unlikely that he would accept a contrary opinion. On reflection, I am inclined to think that any passages which he altered were probably passages about which he already had doubts.

When I had finished playing, he would ask the listeners to say frankly whether they thought it was 'any good' or if he ought to 'throw some of it away'. During the discussion which followed, someone would inevitably say that it was difficult to take in a new work on a first hearing, and therefore perhaps Mr. Douglas would be kind enough to play it through again. V.W.'s immediate response to this was to turn to me and ask: 'Can you spare the time? What about your train back to Tunbridge Wells?' So characteristic of the man to think of others at such an important moment for himself.

In a letter to Michael Kennedy, written after the play-through of the Eighth Symphony, V.W. said: 'I had a jury . . . to sit on my new tune and decide whether I had better go on with it. They decided to put it on the "short list" with the proviso that it wanted a lot more revision (with that I entirely agreed).' The letter shows, I think, a faint note of discouragement which probably explains why, when he took the score away, he spent several months in giving it 'a lot more revision'. While he was doing this, I put in some intensive work on William Walton's new opera *Troilus and Cressida*.

Walton and Other Composers

Throughout the years 1952 to 1955, while working with V.W. on *Sinfonia Antartica*, *Hodie*, and No. 8, I had been concurrently helping Walton with the preparation of the score of *Troilus and Cressida*, and I must say that at times it was rather a tricky business keeping both composers happy, and not letting work for the one interfere with work for the other.

The chief difference between working with V.W. and with Walton is that the latter's manuscript is not so difficult to read. Also, fortunately, Walton apparently does not possess a pocket-knife. One of V.W.'s less endearing habits was that, when he wanted to erase something from an ink-written score, he would take a brutal pocket-knife and scrape the notes away, and with them some of the surface of the paper; he would then write in ink on top of this rough surface, with results which can be surmised. How I would have loved to get my hands on that knife and bury it full fathom five!

When *Troilus* was produced at Covent Garden V.W. went to hear it and 'wished he liked it more'. He decided that perhaps more familiarity might breed content, so he asked me to go and play through the vocal score to him. I agreed, and one morning, to an audience of V.W., Ursula, Gerald Finzi, and another friend, Jean Stewart, I played *and sang* the entire opera.

I'm sorry to say that apparently V.W. didn't like *Troilus* any better when he heard it again in the opera house. This was not because he disliked opera in general, for he greatly admired Wagner and enjoyed Puccini (how many people, I wonder, have detected an unconscious reminiscence of *Madam Butterfly* in the last movement of his Ninth Symphony?) He also loved Verdi and retained a high opinion of the Requiem since his student days.

I have his miniature score of this work, from which he obviously conducted at some time, for it contains many pencilled markings concerned with practical points for rehearsal and indications of his interpretation. I find it curious that although V.W. liked Verdi, who could be very flamboyant and melodramatic at times, he detested the music of Liszt. I have a letter from him which he sent after listening to a broadcast of an arrangement I had made for large orchestra of Liszt's piano work *Funerailles* (its sole performance in twenty years); he wrote: 'I listened to your Liszt – you made the nasty pompous stuff sound almost *noble* – what it must be on the pfte passes my imagination.'

1955: Eighth Symphony Again

At last V.W. finished his revisions of the Eighth Symphony, and on 6 August he wrote: 'Now a new horror! I have decided to finish the symphony and it is all ready for your kind attention whenever you have time and inclination to undertake it.' Three or four days later a further letter said: 'I will send you the symph as soon as I get home at the beginning of October – there is no date fixed – no certainty of a performance – or any rate I imagine not before the spring. It is not a secret – but I think we had better not proclaim it from the house-tops yet.' The last sentence is in answer to my enquiry as to whether I should tell people he had written another symphony; by this time my friends were often asking me, 'What are you doing for V.W. at the moment?' and my replies usually had to be very non-committal.

A few points about the scoring of No. 8 are worth noting. For some reason he intended to use no trombones in this work, but later decided to add them; in October he wrote: 'It was really pure wilfulness which made me leave them out in the first movement because I determined to do without them, though the necessity stared me in the face. You may remember that the original version of the last movement also had no trombones. Harps: I don't want two harps if I can help it. Impresarios do not seem to mind how much percussion they engage [V.W. was wrong there!] but I only know of 2 performances of my *Sea Symphony* in 45 years in which the second harp was used.' (I had suggested that he had written so many notes in the harp part that it should be rewritten for two players.) 'I went to *Turandot* yesterday and they used a set of tuned gongs ... which sounded superb ... much better than tubular bells.' He was so delighted by these gongs that he wrote a part for them in the last movement of No. 8, adding a note saying: 'The gongs are not absolutely essential, but their inclusion is highly desirable.' It was just as well they were not essential, for it was found that the only set of tuned gongs in the country belonged to Covent Garden, and these huge objects had to be transported at great expense to Manchester and elsewhere for any performance where they were to be included. Later he wrote: 'I am in rather a flapdoodle about the new gong part – or rather its notation.' He wanted the gongs if possible instead of tubular bells, but also a gong note of indeterminate pitch; then he decided to have the gongs *and* the bells: 'I rather feel the more the merrier.' At the end of a long and complicated letter he added: 'What a bloody nuisance I am!' Also in No. 8 he wrote an extensive part for the vibraphone, an instrument which I detest – to me it seems more suited to slushy waltz-tunes and mushy love scenes in films; I expressed my dislike to V.W., but he had obviously been captivated by its sound when he used it in *Antartica*.

1956: Manchester Again

I finished work on the 788 bars of the full score of No. 8 at the end of 1955, and on 6 February 1956 V.W., Ursula, and I went to Manchester again, where Barbirolli and the Hallé were to rehearse the work. This time I knew what to expect and, with nine hours of hard labour looming ahead on the following day, I went to bed at about nine o'clock. Not so the youthful composer (he was then in his eighty-fourth year): after dinner he went off to conduct a rehearsal of the *St. Matthew Passion* for a performance which he was due to conduct some time later. The next day he listened to his new symphony for nine hours; and on the following morning he rehearsed the boys' choir for the *Passion* before we caught our train at midday.

His vitality and capacity for hard work were truly astonishing. Ursula – who was forty years his junior – once murmured something to the effect that it was 'difficult to keep up with these young people'; I was thirty-five years younger than he and considered myself fairly tough, but I tired far more quickly than V.W. I recall one occasion about this time, when he had just been conducting a three-hour rehearsal of his *Sea Symphony*, which is a work lasting over an hour, with a large chorus and orchestra to be controlled by the conductor; I said to him: 'Don't you find it tiring, conducting such a big work for so long?' and he replied: 'Oh no, it's easy when you know the tune'. He was probably using the word 'tune' in his usual sense of one of his own works, but the remark shows the calm way in which he could tackle such a daunting task.

During the train journey back to London from Manchester, he produced the full score of No. 8 from his bag, and saying to me 'Could you bear to do a little work?' proceeded to show me a number of pencillings which he had made in the margins, concerning alterations in the scoring and expression marks. After a while, he left me to insert these in my copy of the score, and went happily off to sleep.

A fortnight later he wrote: 'I have had a letter from Alan Frank asking me whether the symphony is ready to print, or whether I want to wait to hear another performance. I feel, at present, that I can pass it with those alterations we made in the train. . . . But you know my mind by this time and do you think it likely that I shall, or do you yourself want other revisions?'

(A postscript by Ursula says: 'What a good thing it was that you took your degree in Foretelling, crystal gazing and Cultivation of Second Sight at Salamanca'.)

Two days after the first London performance came a letter which began: 'I fear you will curse me by all your

gods, but I want one more slight alteration in the symph.'
When this had been dealt with, we at last decided that
the symphony was ready for publication.

After I had finished reading the proofs of No. 8 in
July, most of the rest of my year was taken up with work
on Walton's Cello Concerto. Then in January 1957 I
received a carefully mysterious letter from Alan Frank
which said: 'In the very strictest confidence, I have
elicited vague information from V.W. to the effect that it
is possible that he may ask you to do a job for him in two
or three months' time.' The two or three months
lengthened into seven before I discovered what this job
was to be. In the meantime I finished work on the Walton,
and completed a Suite of my own for string orchestra.
I also edited the vocal score and full score of V.W.'s
Cantata *Epithalamion*, the words of which were chosen
by Ursula from Edmund Spenser's poem. It was founded
on the Masque *The Bridal Day*, which V.W. and Ursula
had written in collaboration some years earlier.

1957-1958: Ninth Symphony

At last, on 5 August 1957, the great secret was revealed;
not 'proclaimed from the house-tops' but announced in
a letter from V.W. telling me that he had completed
some movements of another symphony – the Ninth. I
received this letter on a Monday and in it he asked me
to go up and play three movements to him on the Friday.
This meant that I had to play these movements at sight

from his 'fair copy' of a kind of reduced score – not a true piano arrangement (I used to make the rather desperate joke that what he called a 'fair copy' could often be more accurately described as an 'unfair copy'). On previous occasions he had sent me the music several days in advance, so that I had a chance to decipher the notes before having to play them. Often he would send the full score also, the two copies being wrapped up in a bit of much-used brown paper, tied round with a piece of thin string; the parcels sometimes used to arrive with music poking through at each end. In his modesty he never seemed to realize that posterity might attach some value to his original manuscripts; to him they were apparently merely part of his working material.

When I arrived at Hanover Terrace I asked for half an hour or so to look through what I had to play. This he granted reluctantly, but every few minutes he made some excuse to come into the room to see if I was ready. His eagerness to hear his new 'tune' was so touching that I gave up studying the copy and sat down and played the music to him.

On leaving, I took away the scores of the first two movements in order to make a more playable piano arrangement which for some reason he wanted. Then in October I played the Scherzo and last movement to V.W. and Ursula, and afterwards arranged these movements for piano.

On 2 November I played the complete Ninth Symphony – twice through, as usual – to the 'inner circle' of expert friends; and three days later V.W., Ursula, and I journeyed across London to Malcolm Sargent's flat where I played it to him. He was to conduct the first performance, but he had been too busy to come to V.W.'s house to hear it played there.

After these two play-throughs I started 'washing the face' of the full score, but this was the first – and only – occasion when I was unable to complete a job for V.W. without assistance. An orchestral run-through had been arranged for 21 March 1958, and time ran very short, so John Carewe was called in to help by deciphering and writing out a score of the last movement. He made a good job of this, though he doubtless found it demanding on his ingenuity, patience, and eyesight. I finished checking the band parts two days before the run-through on the 21st, and on the 24th I went to see V.W. about some last-minute alterations he had made; these were finished on the 31st, only just in time for the first hearing on 2 April at the Royal Festival Hall. I say 'first hearing' deliberately rather than 'performance', because this may indicate how intensely I disliked Sargent's version of the Ninth Symphony. He conducted the correct number of beats in the bar efficiently and elegantly, but clearly the nobility and grandeur of the composer's conception meant nothing to him; in particular, he decided that the music was a bit dull in places, so he quickened the speed, but this was just one of many faults in a most unmusicianly account of the entire symphony. My friends sometimes remind me that, as we left the hall, I growled between my teeth: 'Now we can wait for the first performance' – by which I meant that we should not enjoy a truly faithful interpretation of the composer's intentions until we heard the symphony conducted by Adrian Boult, who, in my estimation, is still the finest living conductor of the music of Vaughan Williams. I would mention here that, at the end of 1959, Sir Adrian told me with some anxiety that he found his reading of the Ninth Symphony took about four or five minutes longer than Sargent's; it is typical of his modesty and his lifelong devotion to the cause of interpreting music as the composer would wish, that Sir Adrian should ask me if I thought he might be taking some of it too slowly. I was only too pleased to be able to assure him that it was he who was right.

The Ninth Symphony, incidentally, has a special significance for me, because it is the only work by Vaughan Williams of which I can claim to have composed one note! In the second movement V.W. made a small cut just after figure 21 between what are now the second and third bars; in the first of these bars the solo cello has six quavers, the last of these originally descending to a low B flat; after the cut had been made, this meant an awkward leap up to the treble clef in the next bar. I suggested altering this B flat to the G flat above to make a smoother join; V.W. agreed, and that G flat thus became my sole contribution towards 'writing his music for him'.

1958: Unfinished Works

Less than a week after hearing the Ninth Symphony at the Royal Festival Hall, I was up at Hanover Terrace again, discussing with V.W. a few small amendments to the work. During the morning he told me that he had been writing a new opera, and asked I me if would play some of

D*

it after lunch. Naturally I agreed unhesitatingly, and in the afternoon I played Act I Scene I, while Gil turned the pages and joined me in singing everything within our vocal range and out of it.

This proved to be my last meeting with V.W., and I love to recall the scene which had become so familiar over the years: V.W. leaning back in his armchair, relaxed yet listening intently, with Ursula always close at hand.

During that summer V.W. completed a draft version of the vocal score of the entire opera, but when he died, on 26 August 1958, he had not even started the orchestral score, so – alas – the work remains in an unfinished state. This is particularly to be lamented, for the opera would doubtless have proved an outstandingly interesting and successful achievement, as it was the result of close collaboration with Ursula, who had written the libretto based on the old ballads of Thomas the Rhymer and Tam Lin.

Another work which he did not complete was a Cello Concerto. This exists in a 'fair copy' for cello with a piano version which is virtually a sketch for scoring, but he had not got down to the task of creating the full score, so this work must also be considered as unfinished. And, in my opinion, that is how both of these works should remain, for I strongly disapprove of tampering with unfinished works, especially those of Vaughan Williams. Admittedly Deryck Cooke made a superlative job of his 'performing version' of Mahler's Tenth Symphony, but less scrupulous musicians have made a sorry mess of dishing up the unfinished works of other deceased composers. One can only hope that if in the future some well-meaning meddler is tempted to 'orchestrate in the style of the composer' the unfinished works of Vaughan Williams, he will pause to consider whether he may possibly be insulting the composer's reputation.

It must be emphasized that these early drafts, of *Thomas the Rhymer* and the Cello Concerto, cannot for a moment be regarded as representative of the works as they might have eventually appeared. The composer would have revised them again and again, as he always did his large-scale works. There would have been a second, and perhaps a third, draft and then a fair copy of the piano version; after this he would have made a rough draft of the full score, probably a second draft of some sections, and at last a fair copy of the complete full score. Each time he wrote out one of these versions he would have made changes: in the note values, the rhythmic patterns, the harmonies, the passage work, and of course the scoring. Even some of the tunes might have been altered, for he occasionally reshaped subsidiary themes as a work progressed. It would therefore be grossly unfair to the composer to present these works to the public in their unpolished state, and unpardonable to attempt to 'finish' them.

People have sometimes said to me: 'Why don't you orchestrate these unfinished works? You understand his methods of scoring.' The answer to this is a very firm 'no'. Understanding his methods of scoring – and I am not at all sure I can claim to 'understand' those methods – does not mean that one could successfully orchestrate V.W.'s music in his own inimitable style, most certainly not a symphonic work or an opera. At the back of my mind is always the example of Elgar who, when he realized that he would not live to complete his Third

Symphony, said to W. H. Reed: 'Don't let anybody tinker with it'. As long as I live I am resolved not to tinker with the unfinished major works of Vaughan Williams.

And now, after having expressed myself so uncompromisingly on the subject, I have to confess that I did complete one of V.W.'s unfinished scores; and, as this must seem absurdly inconsistent, I must explain how that happened.

1958: The First Nowell

A Nativity play was to be produced at Drury Lane Theatre in aid of the St. Martin-in-the-Fields Appeal for Refugees, and V.W. had agreed to provide the music. The libretto was adapted by Simona Pakenham from medieval pageants, and the music was almost entirely based on Christmas tunes to which V.W. was giving new settings for soloists and orchestra and new harmonizations for chorus. He had done quite a lot of work on the score, but it was left unfinished, in the middle of a choral setting of 'The First Nowell'. A very difficult problem now had to be faced: should the work be left incomplete and the unfortunate organizers of the performance be told they must find someone else to start writing a fresh score, or was V.W.'s work in a sufficiently advanced state for me to add a few small finishing touches? When I looked through the full score and the sketches, it seemed to me that the orchestration was about three-quarters completed, and there were pencil sketches of the unscored sections – very rough sketches indeed: some of them were not much more than musical-shorthand notes for the eye of the composer only.

A decision had to be made fairly quickly, and Ursula, Simona, Gil, and I gave much anxious thought to the matter. We eventually agreed in thinking that Vaughan Williams himself would not have liked the idea of dis-appointing the organizers of the appeal for this worthy charitable cause; it was therefore decided that I should attempt to do what was necessary to complete the score.

As soon as I started work on it, however, I realized that there was far more to be done than I had estimated; for instance, the most spectacular scene in the production was the procession of the Three Kings with their long retinues, for which V.W. had planned a slow, march-like movement based on the choral 'How brightly shines the morning star'. When I came to deal with this I found there was nothing but an extremely scratchy-looking sixty-bar sketch in his most illegible handwriting, some of the bars containing nothing but the tune of the choral, the harmonies not having been filled in. This I had to decipher and expand into a four-minute movement for full chorus and orchestra. Later on it was discovered that certain aspects of the stage presentation required extra short sections of music – a few bars here and there to be tacked on to the beginnings and endings of the pieces V.W. had already written. Here I found myself in a very tricky position indeed: I had perforce to compose several brief passages of imitation Vaughan Williams music. I was acutely conscious of the fact that, unless I was extremely careful, these imitations might turn out to be almost like tasteless parodies of certain little mannerisms of his style, and I wanted so desperately to do this job sincerely, and not to do anything of which he might have been ashamed. Had I realized that I would be confronted by such an extraordinarily difficult problem, I doubt whether I would have had the courage to take on the task. I trust I shall not be thought guilty of immoderate self-satisfaction when I add that nowadays, when I look at some of these joined-on passages, I find it very hard to detect exactly where my imitations end and the authentic Vaughan Williams music starts. This comforts me more than a little, and I mention it here in the hope that it may perhaps be considered as evidence that my only attempt at completing one of V.W.'s scores was seemingly not unpardonable. In further justification of my action I must point out that the completion of a collection of arrangements of traditional tunes – as this was – is a very different proposition from the attempted completion of an opera or a concerto.

The work was given the title of *The First Nowell*, and the O.U.P. agreed to my earnest request that, when the vocal score was published, each section should be clearly marked as being 'by R.V.W.', or 'by R.D.', or 'completed by R.D.', to make quite sure that posterity would not 'blame him for my shortcomings'.

In conversation with Frank Howes before the first performance I said that I had completed the score from 'first sketches, second drafts, third thoughts, and semi-final scores,' a phrase which he thought worth quoting in *The Times*. In his press notice after the performance he said: 'The harmonizations bear the unmistakable mark of Vaughan Williams, though the score had to be completed by Roy Douglas, who knew Vaughan Williams's mind and, perhaps a rarer accomplishment, could read his hand-writing.'

One manuscript full score in my possession is prized above all others: this is V.W.'s uncompleted score of *The First Nowell*. There I recognize the familiar sights: the bar-lines drawn with a single stroke of the pen – surprisingly near to being straight – without the aid of a ruler; the numerous alterations; the frequent use of that abominable pocket-knife; the bits stuck on (crooked) with sticky tape; the occasional ink blot; a mistransposition in the clarinet part; a couple of bars for the horn written on the bassoon line; a change of time-signature omitted. Most affecting of all is page 42. He had obviously decided that, before finishing some of the earlier sections, he would score the last movement, a new version of 'The First Nowell' for chorus and orchestra. At one of his private carol parties he had discovered that 'The First Nowell goes in canon', and he was no doubt delightedly arranging the third verse in this manner, the lower half of the chorus and orchestra starting a bar after the upper half. On page 41 he had reached the words 'And by the light of that same star Three Wise Men came from. . . .' One turns the page. There are the names of the instruments in the left-hand margin, and nothing else. I still find myself deeply moved when I look at this empty page.

1958-1962: Sorting the Manuscripts

The story of my personal association with Vaughan Williams is now completed, and the fact must regretfully be faced that from this point the principal figure will seldom appear in the narrative. Nevertheless, my association with his music has continued almost uninterruptedly until the present day, and I think it worth while to give an account of my varied activities since 1958 in connection with his works, for this will show that – in spite of a short period of being out of fashion with superior people – the music of Vaughan Williams has never lost its place in the affections of the music-loving public. The truth of this assertion is evidenced by the large number of scores and recordings which have been issued during the past few years, for music publishers and recording companies do not go to the trouble and expense of issuing the works of a composer whose music is no longer wanted.

For the past thirteen years my work has been done on a large and solid table of the type found in a solicitor's office; it is five feet wide, just over three feet deep, with massive carved legs. This is the table on which V.W. wrote most of his music for many years, surrounded by his much-loved cats. When Ursula invited me in 1958 to take on the job of sorting out all the manuscripts, I accepted the task with keen interest, though not without some misgivings as to the magnitude of the undertaking. On 1 October she took me to this table and opened a drawer. It was two feet wide, eighteen inches deep, and three inches high; in the drawer were two piles of manuscripts reaching to the top: MSS of 1958, 1925, 1943 – in fact, MSS from almost every period of his musically prolific life. Some were turned inside out, some were merely pages torn from scores, and occasionally a few sheets of one work were tucked into another. After I had spent some time in trying to identify these and sort them out, Ursula said: 'You do realize there's another drawer beside this one, don't you?' I had not realized it, but there it was, similarly packed with MSS. And, while I was coping with these, she broke the news gently that there were two more drawers at the far side of the table.

Some weeks later, I was taken to the boxroom, where there were three trunks and a suitcase, also stuffed full of manuscripts. All these, too, had to be identified and sorted out, and the more important items labelled before they were sent to the British Museum, to which they were presented by Ursula. Many visits were paid to Hanover Terrace during 1959 before I completed this long and often bewildering and mentally exhausting task. It was, of course, extremely interesting to go through the accumulation of a lifetime's musical creation. Many of the works were very familiar, some I had never even heard of, and others were very early works which he had not thought worthy of publication: these he was presumably keeping in case he wanted to make use of some of the tunes, as he had occasionally done with other tunes from discarded works.

We made a few happy discoveries, one being a *Suite de Ballet* for flute and piano. This had been copied out by V.W. in such an unusually clear and tidy handwriting that it was permissible, I am sure, to assume that at one time he may have thought of having it published. My guess was that he had been keeping it back until he had time to add some expression marks, for there were only two or three in the copy. I added a few more where I thought they seemed fairly obvious, and we decided that we could take it upon ourselves to allow it to be published, with the stipulation that all my added expression marks were to be enclosed in brackets, with a foot-note stating that they were R.D.'s and not the composer's; this was for his sake, not mine. There was also a *Romance* for viola and piano, with no clues as to when it was written; we decided that this, too, could be published.

These decisions, as to whether a work should be submitted for publication or not, were taken by Ursula, Gil, Michael, and me, after much earnest consideration, separately and together. On similar occasions in later years we were sometimes joined in our deliberations by Elizabeth Maconchy, or some other musician of experience and integrity who had known and loved V.W. The final decision regarding publication always rested, of course, with Alan Frank, as Head of Music of the O.U.P. There was never any hesitation on his part, however, for Alan, as well as being a practical man and an experienced musician, had been a friend of V.W.'s and a devoted admirer of his music.

In a trunk in the boxroom I discovered a song; this, like the *Suite de Ballet*, had been copied by V.W. in a remarkably neat handwriting – far better than anything I had ever had to deal with! It was labelled *Songs of Travel* No. 9: 'I have trod the upward and the downward slope'. When I showed this to Ursula she was delighted, for the existence of this song had been known, but it had been mislaid for many years. A copy was sent to Boosey and Hawkes, the publishers of the other *Songs of Travel*, and they were at last able to issue the complete cycle in the order in which the composer wished the songs to be sung. This 'little epilogue', as V.W. had described it on his copy, quotes some of the earlier songs in the cycle, and thus rounds it off to perfection.

When I had finished the task of sorting out the manuscripts, I assumed that my long association with the music of Vaughan Williams had now come to an end, but this supposition proved to be entirely wrong. First I had to tidy up a few of his later works which were almost ready, and intended by him, for publication; such as the *Three Vocalises* for soprano and clarinet, and the *Four Last Songs*, lovely settings of poems by Ursula. With these it was merely a matter of providing readable copies for the engraver, and – in the case of the *Four Last Songs* – adding a few expression marks in brackets.

Then the vocal score of *The First Nowell* had to be prepared for publication, and an arrangement of the score made for strings with organ or piano. This was followed by a cued-in version of V.W.'s own orchestration of the *Prelude to 49th Parallel*, and an adaptation of this for string orchestra; a new and corrected score to be made of the *Magnificat*; and a number of smaller jobs of editing, correcting, and proof-reading.

1962: Pilgrim's Journey

In 1962 the Rev. G. J. Cuming suggested to O.U.P. that, as it did not seem likely that *Pilgrim's Progress* would be performed on the stage very often, and as this meant that a wealth of glorious music would therefore be lying on the shelves unheard, it might be a good idea to construct a cantata for concert performance out of some of the most beautiful and suitable sections. Christopher Morris (the O.U.P. Music Editor) and I consulted Ursula about this, and it was agreed that we should go ahead with the scheme. We decided to call it *Pilgrim's Journey*, and the choice of movements was made by Christopher – who also did some clever dovetailing of some of the sections – and myself.

The first performance was at Dorking, but it was the second performance (the world deuxième?) which gave me more pleasure. This was given in Tunbridge Wells by singers from the County Grammar School for Girls and the Skinners' School for Boys. These youngsters sang with great enthusiasm and variety of colour, and with astonishing ease considering the complexity of some of the choral writing. Knowing V.W.'s special affection for the music-makings of young people, I am sure he would have much enjoyed their performance.

At this point I must pay a warm personal tribute to Christopher Morris, who combines admirable musician-ship with a very practical attention to details; ever since he joined the O.U.P. we have consulted together on countless musical problems, and have almost invariably agreed thereon. The friendly co-operation of Christopher has contributed largely towards making my years of working for the O.U.P. (I have never been a member of the staff) pleasant and artistically rewarding. A con-siderable debt is owed to him by lovers of the music of Vaughan Williams – and of many other British composers – for the infinite care he invariably takes to ensure that the music is presented on paper as the composer con-ceived it in his mind.

Another interesting task which I undertook in 1962 was for Boosey and Hawkes. In 1905 V.W. had orchestrated the accompaniments of the three most famous of his *Songs of Travel* – 'The Vagabond', 'Bright is the Ring of Words', and 'The Roadside Fire' – and Booseys asked me to orchestrate the remaining six. The problem here was: should I score them in my own style (the answer was clearly no), in the style of the orchestrations he had made in 1905, or in the way he might have scored them in 1958 (which would have been vastly different)? The final result was a typically British compromise, but I took care to use in my scoring only those instruments which he had used in 1905. In 1968 I arranged a string orchestra accompaniment for five of the songs. Perhaps I should make the point clear that such orchestrations of already published music are not to be thought of as 'tampering with unfinished works'; they are more to be classed with the orchestral versions which R.V.W. himself made of works by Meyerbeer and others – not to mention some of the very unconventional additions he made to some of Bach's scores!

It was also in 1962 that I began to get involved with the two books which were being written about Vaughan Williams: Ursula's biography and Michael Kennedy's exhaustive and authoritative volume on the music. Earlier, in 1960, I had much enjoyed playing through to Michael most of V.W.'s very early works, some dating back as far as the 1890s, and then discussing them with him in detail. From 1962 until 1964 I read both books in first and second manuscript, in first and second typescript, and eventually in proof. So I knew quite a lot about these books before they were published – with the exception of one page which was kept back from me until I received a printed copy of Michael's book: this was the page on which he had dedicated it to me. I was very touched by this gesture on Michael's part.

1965-1972: *Work Still in Progress*

During the past few years most of my work on the music of Vaughan Williams has been concerned with previously unpublished full scores. For those enthusiasts who enjoy studying music in print, small scores of V.W.'s better known major works have been on sale for a long time, but the less frequently performed works have not been published in small score form, and have been obtainable only on hire. In recent years the O.U.P. have been publishing study scores of some of these less familiar works.

Each time they decide to issue one of these, a copy of the full score from the hire library is sent to me for 'face washing' before it is given to the engraver. The copy is often one written in the 1920s or 1930s by a professional copyist who no doubt did his best but was not entirely successful in interpreting V.W.'s manuscript accurately; consequently there are small mistakes on almost every page. Also, during its lifetime the score has probably been hired out many times to conductors who have made marks all over it with thick coloured pencils (thereby obliterating some of the notes), and have mis-corrected some of the mistakes, thus adding to the confusion. I compare this score with another copy – which perhaps contains different mistakes; then with the band parts –

which sometimes disagree with the scores; then with a
piano score – which only reveals further discrepancies;
then, if possible, with the original MS – which usually
makes matters worse. Finally I have to use my own
judgement, based on my experience in dealing with
similar problems during my work with the composer;
in short, it is my job to decide for posterity what V.W.
really meant to put on paper forty or fifty years ago. It is
quite a heavy responsibility, and one which I must admit
I find rather worrying at times, especially when I realize
that there is no one in the world to whom I can apply for
an authoritative decision if I am unable to make up my
mind on some particular teaser. On such occasions I
usually discuss the point with Christopher Morris, and
together we find a solution.

Among the scores I have helped to prepare for publica-
tion are: the Viola Suite, the Oboe Concerto, *Hodie*,
Benedicite, *In the Fen Country*, *Dona Nobis Pacem*, *Five
Tudor Portraits*, the Concerto for Two Pianos, *An Oxford
Elegy* (the vocal score), *Norfolk Rhapsody*, *Fantasia on the
Old 104th*, and *Riders to the Sea*.

During my cleaning up operations there is one problem
which constantly arises: discrepancies between the published piano copies and the unpublished full scores. As I
have described earlier, V.W. would often make considerable changes in the actual music while he was scoring a
work; unfortunately, he seldom bothered to make these
changes in the piano sketch from which he was working.
Then, much later, after the work had been performed,
the O.U.P. would ask him to provide a piano copy to
serve as a basis for publication, and it is now quite clear
to me that he would nearly always send them his piano

sketch for this purpose – completely forgetting that it did not contain any of the changes!

I had already encountered this problem in 1951 when I was checking the proofs of the vocal score of *Pilgrim's Progress*; in this instance he had obviously sent, for the use of the engraver, his rough piano sketches (which were more like a short score), with the result that there are a large number of discrepancies between the printed vocal score and the full score, and in many places the distribution of the notes between the hands is far from pianistic. By the time the vocal score reached me in proof stage, it was far too late for me to start making drastic changes.

The works in which these discrepancies appear most often are the operas and choral works, especially those which he dealt with when I was not at hand to keep an eye on what was happening! And it was these discrepancies which led to much of the confusion in the full scores. Over the years, conductors and performers would 'correct' the full score to make it agree with the piano copy, then other conductors would 'correct' the score again to make it agree with the orchestral parts, then others would 'correct' the parts to agree with the mis-corrected full score – and very few of these well-intentioned people would think of telling the O.U.P. what they had done. So the perplexing muddles did not come to light until I examined the full scores in detail when preparing them for publication.

In October 1970 I was asked to check the vocal score of *Sir John in Love* in readiness for its being reprinted. I compared it with the full score in the hire library, and the more I looked, the more disorder I found. Clearly, each time V.W. had heard the opera he had made changes

– some small and some quite drastic – and these had been
made in the full score (and usually in the band parts,
though not always) but not in the vocal score because that
was already published. Four years after the opera's first
performance he had added a Prologue, Episode, and
Interlude (he later withdrew the Prologue); a vocal score
of these three sections was printed separately, and it is
now only on hire. In this vocal score, the Interlude is
labelled: 'to be played between scenes I and II of Act II,
or between Acts I and II'; but, when I looked at the full
score, there I found the Interlude in V.W.'s own writing
inserted and labelled by him as Act III Scene I! The
confusion was worse confounded, of course, because the
Interlude does not appear at all in the published vocal
score of the 'complete' opera. In addition to getting all
this straightened out, I had to rewrite over a hundred
pages of the full score, because some pages had been
altered so much that they were unintelligible, and others
were photographed copies of the composer's far from
best handwriting. I solved the last of the problems and
inserted the final corrections for the reprint of the vocal
score in July 1971.

Answering Queries

And now, thirty years after that first skirmish with his
remarkable handwriting in the scores of *Coastal Command*,
my table – his table, which has so many memories for
me – is seldom without at least one of the works of

Vaughan Williams sitting on it, either a full score waiting for me to 'wash its face' for the engraver, or a pile of proofs to be checked. What is more, I seem to have reached the position – the sometimes decidedly unenviable position – of being considered the ultimate authority on the music of Vaughan Williams, for I am called upon to provide answers to an extraordinary variety of questions which come from many parts of the world: whether 'on the third quaver in the eleventh bar of the third movement' of one of the symphonies 'the second violins should have an A natural or an A flat'; whether it would be all right for a male voice choir to perform a work which V.W. had written for mixed chorus, by letting the tenors sing the soprano part an octave lower; whether a large-scale work for chorus and full orchestra could be done by a choir of thirty with an organ, a trumpet, a trombone, a tuba, and timpani – these are actual examples of the queries which are passed on to me for a decisive answer.

One question which crops up from time to time concerns his metronome marks: should these be faithfully observed or not? Conscientious performers set their metronomes to markings such as crotchet equals 186 or crotchet equals 48, and find to their dismay that the one is impracticably fast and the other too slow to be musically convincing. The answer to the question is implicit, I think, in the fact that V.W. did not possess a metronome! It would therefore be reasonable to assume that his marking should be taken as an indication of the mood of the piece, rather than as a numerical certainty. Also, it is worth mentioning that there is some evidence that the speed marked at the beginning of a movement was not always intended by him to be maintained unchanged throughout. Sometimes, while I was playing one of his works to him, he would make gentle conducting motions with his hand to show me that he wanted the music to move a little faster or slower, although there was nothing in the copy to indicate this. Such modifications of pace were occasionally noticeable when he conducted his own works.

A non-technical question which I have been asked is: was V.W. a good teacher? This I am unable to answer as I was never a pupil of his, but from what I have been told he enjoyed teaching, and his pupils worshipped him. On an earlier page I have quoted him as saying he did not like 'young men from the College who think they know everything'. It must not be deduced from this remark that he disapproved of colleges of music and their products, or that he despised academic training. On the contrary: it was his firm opinion that a composer should learn his job thoroughly in order to be a true master of his craft; it might be said that he approved of academies but disliked academicism. No 'warbling his native wood-notes wild' for V.W.; a more appropriate quotation from his admired Milton would be: 'By labour and intent study . . . joined with the strong propensity of nature, I might perhaps leave something so written to after-times, as they should not willingly let it die.'

Epilogue

What have I failed to say about V.W.? In recording these inevitably personal memories, I am conscious that I have not done justice to many of the qualities of that great and lovable man. My aim has been to show some aspects of his personality of which I was particularly aware, and I have tried to avoid going over the ground which Ursula Vaughan Williams and Michael Kennedy have already covered with such loving care. Something will have emerged, I hope, of his extraordinary modesty about his music, his ever-questing desire to learn, his irrepressible sense of humour, and his unfailing thoughtfulness for others.

One thing I have not made clear is that, while I was spending months in the preparation of his major works, he was usually busy composing smaller works, a large number of which were performed and published without my assistance. The fertility of his musical imagination was amazing – once he began composing a new 'tune' the music just poured from him in such abundance that his pen could scarcely write fast enough to get it down on paper. This was, of course, part of the reason for his indecipherable handwriting. On reflection, I think we must be very glad that he wrote so fast and so illegibly: had he written more slowly, we should obviously have had fewer of the works of Vaughan Williams to give us lasting pleasure. And, from an entirely personal point of view: had his handwriting been easier to read, he might never have discovered that I could be helpful to him, and from that it follows that I should not have eventually enjoyed his friendship, and my musical life would never have been enriched by the unforgettable and infinitely precious experience of working with R.V.W.